DISCOVERING
OUR HERITAGE

ARGENTINA
A WILD WEST HERITAGE

BY MARGE AND ROB PETERSON
REVISED EDITION BY
MARGE PETERSON

DILLON PRESS
PARSIPPANY, NEW JERSEY

Acknowledgements

For help in preparing the written portions of this book, as well as the photographs, the authors would like to thank the cultural affairs division of the Argentine embassy, Susanna Bono, Victoria Engstrom, Roy Bean, Sam Lunt, Kloyd Donaldson, Dennis Payne, Alfredo Bono, and Ruben Vgartemendía. We would especially like to thank our editor at Dillon Press, Lora Lee Polack.

Photo Credits
(Photo credits from previous edition)
Photos have been reproduced through the courtesy of E. M. Fisher; Luis Martin, J. Halber/D. Donne Bryant Photography; Chip and Rosa Maria Peterson; Inter-American Development Bank; Graham Harris; Travel Image; Organization of American States; Museum of Latin American Art; Carl L. Newsom; CBS Television; S. Bono; A. Bono; R. Vgartemendía; M. Peterson and the San Martín Society; and UN Photo 172246/J. Izaac (p. 113).

(Second edition photo credits)
Front Cover: Map, Ortelius Design. Chip & Rosa María de la Cueva Peterson; Wenger International/© Pardo.
Marge Peterson: 31, 81, 92. SBG: 5. Map, Ortelius Design: 6.

Library of Congress Cataloging-in-Publication Data

Peterson, Marge.
    Argentina : a wild west heritage / by Marge and Bob Peterson ;
revised edition by Marge Peterson. --2nd ed.
       p.   cm. -- (Discovering our heritage)
    Includes bibliographical references and index.
    Summary: Describes the people, culture, geography, history, festivals, and attractions of Argentina.
    ISBN 0-382-39287-6 (lsb)
    1. Argentina--Juvenile literature.   [1. Argentina.]
I. Peterson, Rob.   II. Title.   III. Series.
F2808.2.P48   1997
982—dc20   95-49075

Cover and book design By Michelle Farinella

Published by Dillon Press
A Division of Simon & Schuster
299 Jefferson Road, Parsippany, NJ 07054

Second edition
Printed in the United States of America
10 9 8 7 6 5 4 3 2 1

CONTENTS

Fast Facts about Argentina

Official Name: *República Argentina* (Argentine Republic).

Capital: Buenos Aires.

Location: Argentina is located in southern South America. It is bordered by Bolivia and Paraguay to the north, Chile to the west, Brazil and Uruguay to the northeast, and the Atlantic Ocean to the east.

Area: 1,065,189 square miles (2,731,253 square kilometers). *Greatest distances*—north-south, 2,300 miles (3,700 kilometers); east-west, 980 miles (1,577 kilometers). *Atlantic coastline*—2,500 miles (4,032 kilometers).

Elevation: *Highest*—Mount Aconcagua, 22,831 feet (6,959 meters). *Lowest*—Valdés Peninsula, 131 feet (40 meters) below sea level.

Population: *Estimated 1994 population*—33,900,000. *Distribution*—80 percent of the people live in or near cities; 20 percent live in rural areas. *Density* 30 persons per square mile (12 per square kilometer).

Form of Government: Republic. *Head of Government*—president.

Important Products: *Agriculture*—beef, beef products, fish, wheat, corn, soybeans, grapes, flaxseed, sunflower seeds, sorghum, wool. *Manufacturing*—machinery, automobiles, textiles, steel, railroad cars, chemicals, food products.

Basic Unit of Money: Peso.

Official Language: Spanish.

Major Religions: More than 90 percent of Argentines are Roman Catholic; 2 percent are Protestant, and 2 percent are Jewish.

Flag: Two blue horizontal stripes on either side of a white stripe. On the white stripe at the flag's center is a sun, a symbol of Argentina's freedom from Spain.

National Anthem: *"Himno Nacional Argentino"* ("The National Hymn of Argentina").

Major Holidays: New Year's Day—January 1; Day of the Kings—January 6; Carnival—about six weeks before Easter; Good Friday; Easter Sunday; Labor Day—May 1; Anniversary of the 1810 Revolution—May 25; Independence Day—July 9; Anniversary of the Death of General José de San Martín—August 17; Christmas Day—December 25.

A SILVERY LAND

Four centuries ago, Spanish explorers searched eagerly for silver in a promising but unexplored land in South America. Though silver was never found there in great quantities, the area is known to this day by the Spanish name *Argentina*, or "silvery land."

Present-day Argentina can count natural riches other than silver. Among its varied landscapes are a gigantic fertile plain with some of the world's richest farmland, jagged mountain ranges that hold mineral wealth, and humid rain forests with an exotic array of rare animals and plants.

Another one of Argentina's riches is her people. Most are middle class, enjoying one of the highest standards of living in South America. Argentines value education; a higher percentage of them can read and write than can populations of most countries in the world. Recent times have been good for many Argentines. Even without the silver that the early European explorers craved, Argentina is in many ways a "silvery land."

A Triangle of Land

Argentina is located in the long tail of the continent of South America; its shape is a triangle pointing south. A

*Two young men climb the rocky shores of Lake Hahuel Huapi,
at the foot of the southern Andes Mountains in Argentina.*

huge country, it is four times the size of Texas and is the eighth-largest country in the world. In South America, only Brazil is larger.

Argentina's borders are formed by natural barriers. The Atlantic Ocean washes the country's eastern shores, while to the west stands another commanding barrier, the towering Andes Mountains. This series of giant peaks runs down the South American continent like a spine. For centuries, these forbidding mountains halted or slowed contact between South American peoples to the east and west of them. In this way, the Andes affected Argentine history, and they still affect travel and commerce today.

Argentina shares the tail of South America with its neighbor Chile, which lies on the western side of the Andes Mountains. To the north are Bolivia and Paraguay, separated from Argentina by mountains, scrub forests, floodplains, and swamps. Brazil and Uruguay border Argentina to the northeast.

Most of Argentina has a temperate climate with four distinct seasons—a warm summer, a mild winter with occasional light snowfalls, and a pleasant fall and springtime. Because Argentina is in the Southern Hemisphere, its seasons are the opposite of those in North America, with winter in June, July, and August, and summer in December, January, and February.

The climate at the far ends of the country varies from very cold to very hot. The southern mountains have heavy snowfalls and intense cold, with no real summer. Northern Argentina is hot—tropical in places—without marked changes in seasons.

More than 33 million people live in Argentina, but the population is not spread evenly over the country. One third lives in Buenos Aires, the capital city, and its suburbs. Other parts of the country, particularly the Andes Mountains and the southern region, are thinly populated because living conditions are harsher there.

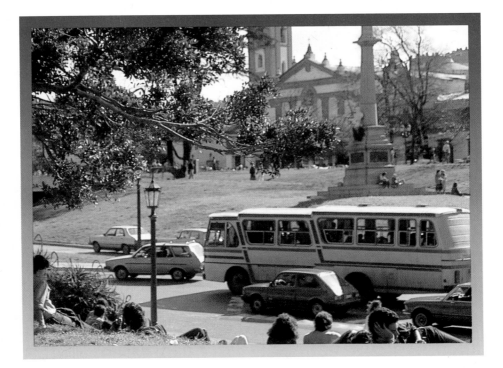

One third of all Argentines live in the bustling capital city of Buenos Aires and its suburbs.

The Northern Lowlands

Northern Argentina is an area of lowlands that covers two distinct regions, Mesopotamia and the Gran Chaco. Mesopotamia lies between the Paraná and Uruguay rivers in the northeast. It was named after a rich kingdom in the ancient Middle East, and it is a land of swamps, rain forests, and rolling grassy plains with no dry season. Heavy rains cause rivers to flood and wash soil southwestward through the river system. In places, the plains have soil 20 feet (6 meters) deep, where farmers grow citrus

Palm trees grow in the grassy plains of Mesopotamia,
a lowland region in northern Argentina.

fruits and *yerba mate*, a holly shrub whose leaves are used
for a popular tea.

In the rain forest of Mesopotamia, the soil is red clay.
Orchids and other plants cling to trees and bloom in the
hot, moist air. The dense jungle is home to howler
monkeys, toucans, parrots, hummingbirds, giant anteaters,
jaguars, and wild pigs.

A rainbow shines through the mist at Iguazú Falls, on the border between Argentina and Brazil.

On Argentina's border with Brazil, the twisting Iguazú River spills over jagged rocks and plunges more than 200 feet (61 meters) to the rocks below. The horseshoe-shaped Iguazú Falls are more than 2 miles (3.2 kilometers) wide, larger than Niagara Falls in the United States. Torrents of water from the 275 individual falls strike the rocks and burst into foamy waters and mist as the river travels southward through a narrow crack named the Devil's Throat.

The Gran Chaco is located east of the Andes Mountains and northwest of Mesopotamia. It is a broad low floodplain, covered mostly with dense scrub forests. This floodplain is shared by Argentina, Brazil, Paraguay, and Bolivia; it is being slowly built up with gravel and silt washed down from the Andes during flooding by the area's many rivers. The Paraguay and the Pilcomayo rivers, which form Argentina's border with Paraguay, are major rivers in the region.

In the Gran Chaco, dry winters alternate with hot, rainy summers, but the moisture evaporates quickly in the heat. Farmers must work steadily to keep fields of cotton, soybeans, and sunflower seeds irrigated. The *quebracho* tree grows here, too. Its wood is so hard that it has earned the name Ax Breaker.

Mountain Peaks and Piedmonts

The Andean region stretches along the entire western border of Argentina. It includes the Andes Mountains and the piedmont, a region at the foot of the mountains. The piedmont in the far northwest is a cold, dry desert at a high elevation. Along the piedmont and in the mountain valleys are cattle ranches, citrus and vegetable farms, and plantations of sugarcane and tobacco. Salta, Tucumán, Córdoba, and San Salvador de Jujuy are old cities in the northwestern piedmont. This area was the first part of Argentina settled by the Spanish in the sixteenth century.

In the central Argentine Andes, where the peaks are sharper and the valleys deeper, stands Mount Aconcagua. At 22,831 feet (6,959 meters), Aconcagua is the tallest peak in the Western Hemisphere. Grapes for Argentina's large winemaking industry grow in dry valleys in the region, with the runoff from melting mountain snows providing irrigation. To the south of Aconcagua is an important mountain pass between Argentina and Chile, once used by Incas and Spanish explorers. Today, the Uspallata Pass can be crossed by train or by car on sharply curving roads which must be closed during fierce winter snowstorms. The pass is marked by a huge statue, "Christ of the Andes," which honors the peaceful relations between Argentina and Chile.

As the Andes Mountains reach farther south, they lose height but are still capped with snow. Glaciers stretch over wide areas between mountains. Streams fed by melting glacier ice have salmon and trout; flamingos and blacknecked swans feed in lagoons. In the Andean foothills live pumas; Patagonian hares; and *guanacos*, small, humpless relatives of the camel. Tourism is important to the economy of this region.

A Sea of Grass

The heart of Argentina is the Pampa, an endless sea

A small herd of wild guanacos graze on shrubs near the coast of southern Argentina.

of tall grass that covers the land for hundreds of miles. The Spanish explorers, thinking these plains worthless, hurried across them to search elsewhere for silver. Today, the fertile Pampa is Argentina's foodbasket and provides wealth from export sales of wheat, sorghum, corn, soybeans, sunflower seeds, and flaxseeds. More than two out of every three Argentines live on the Pampa, which covers one fifth of the country.

The Pampa is nourished by moderate temperatures and adequate rainfalls, although eastern areas nearer the seacoast tend to get more rain than areas in the west. At times, violent windstorms called *pamperos* move

suddenly across the Pampa, bringing downpours of rain with violent thunder and lightning displays.

The constant breezes of the western Pampa turn windmills, which pump water for vast herds of cattle. Farms and ranches—large and small—are fenced in now, but at one time, Argentine cowhands, called gauchos, drove huge herds of cattle across unfenced lands. Today modern gauchos of the Pampa might earn a living by operating a combine to harvest wheat, driving a tractor to plant grain seeds, or working on guest ranches where visitors experience the gaucho lifestyle.

Grain and livestock products are shipped abroad through several ports on the Pampa's edge. Santa Fe and Rosario are on the Paraná River, and Buenos Aires, the country's chief port, sits on an inlet of the Atlantic Ocean called the Río de la Plata. Farther south along the Atlantic is Bahía Blanca, an ocean port with a deep channel, where dockworkers load and unload the largest ships. Another important seaport is Mar del Plata, a fishing community and popular resort town.

Patagonia

The lower quarter of Argentina is named Patagonia. It is a series of windswept plateaus crossed by deep canyons that flood during the winter rains and dry out during the

A rancher checks his wheat crop in Argentina's fertile Pampa region.

brief summer. Less than three percent of all Argentines live in this chilly, foggy, windy region, which stretches from the Atlantic coast west to the Andes Mountains. Patagonia includes Argentina's part of the island of Tierra del Fuego at the southern tip of the continent. Except for an ice-covered section of Antarctica which Argentina claims, Tierra del Fuego is the southernmost part of the country.

Near the Río Negro in northern Patagonia, farmers grow apples and pears in irrigated orchards, but in general, the grassy plateaus of Patagonia are suitable for just one kind of animal: sheep. Millions of sheep are raised on ranches with only a few farmhands to feed and shear the huge flocks. The region also has oil, aluminum, and rich mineral deposits, much of which are undeveloped.

South of the Río Negro, the Valdés Peninsula juts out into the Atlantic Ocean. A wide variety of animals and seabirds come to this wildlife sanctuary to bear their young because they are not able to land easily elsewhere on Patagonia's rocky, wind-whipped beaches. Penguins, elephant seals, and antarctic doves share the rocks, while whales feed offshore. Inland animals include ostrich-like rheas, gray foxes, armadillos, guanacos, and short-eared rabbits called mara.

More than a thousand miles farther south, large condors sometimes circle over Ushuaia, the southernmost town in the world. This frontier town of 11,000 hardy

Ushuaia, the southernmost town in the world, is located on Tierra del Fuego.

people is on the island of Tierra del Fuego. In Spanish, *Tierra del Fuego* means "Land of Fire." The island earned its name because early explorers saw Indian campfires on its shores. Tierra del Fuego is cold and windy, with snow-covered mountain peaks rising inland. Most of its residents work on the area's prosperous cattle farms or in its sawmills or fishing industry.

A European-Looking Capital

Buenos Aires, Argentina's capital, is surrounded on three sides by the Pampa and on the other side by the Río

Modern high-rise buildings along Corrientes Avenue in busy downtown Buenos Aires

de la Plata. The Paraná and Uruguay rivers empty into this wide estuary just north of the city. The Río de la Plata, or River of Silver, was named by Spanish explorers who came to Argentina looking for the precious metal, but today the muddy water looks more tan than silver.

An international, industrial city, Buenos Aires and its suburbs are busy with the activities of 12 million residents. Although Spain controlled the city for more than 200 years, Buenos Aires doesn't reflect very much of its Spanish heritage. Many buildings are

French in design and were built at the end of the nineteenth century, long after Argentina became independent of Spain.

In today's Buenos Aires, historic buildings stand alongside modern high-rise apartment houses, especially on the broad avenues in the center of the city. In the suburbs are middle and upperclass neighborhoods, as well as crowded slums called *villas miserias*, or "towns of misery," which house the poor.

Because Buenos Aires is a world seaport, its residents are called *porteños*—meaning "people from the port." Ships from around the world dock in the port district, and the Río de la Plata must be continually dredged to remain deep enough to accommodate them. Giant cranes load and unload the shipments that make up Argentina's trade with its major trading partners—the United States, Japan, Brazil, Bolivia, Germany, Italy, and the Netherlands.

Significant differences can be found between the lives of porteños and the lives of rural citizens. Because one out of every three Argentines lives in Buenos Aires or its suburbs, the city is powerful in politics. Funds for roads, schools, and transportation have often been given to Buenos Aires rather than to the countryside. Rural Argentines have sometimes believed that the capital does not consider their needs important; in the past, this feeling has led to economic wars between rural

residents and porteños. Today a little of that friction remains between the two sets of people.

A South American Melting Pot

Argentina is a melting pot of immigrant peoples—not of different races as much as of different nationalities. A half-truthful saying is, "The typical Argentine is an Italian who speaks Spanish and thinks he's British!" Most Argentine people have European ancestors, with the majority from Spanish and Italian backgrounds. These immigrants brought their religion with them, and today Argentina is a Roman Catholic nation. The country was also settled by British, German, Jewish, and other ethnic groups. Even today, some areas have "pocket communities" where an ethnic language is spoken at home and Spanish, the official language, is spoken in public.

Most South American countries have large populations of *mestizos*, people of mixed European and Indian background, but Argentina does not. Argentina's mestizo population is small, yet its Indian population is even smaller. Many native Argentine Indians died of diseases, such as measles, brought by the Europeans who settled the land, but many more were killed in the late nineteenth century by settlers who wanted Indian lands for farming and ranching.

Like this young boy, many Argentinians have the tan skin and brown hair typical of their southern European ancestors.

Defeating Inflation

Although Argentina had for more than 50 years a stormy political history, with a series of military dictators ruling the nation, in 1983 the country returned to a democratically elected civilian government. Recently, Argentina has been enjoying political stability and economic prosperity. In the first half of the 1990s the nation won a hard-fought battle with inflation—an old enemy that kept many families from affording adequate housing and food. Governmental economic reforms have pushed inflation to a fifty-year low. Argentina has also succeeded in becoming a stronger trading partner with other nations.

Still, Argentina has worries. The poorest people have not been helped as much as others by the economic changes of the past decade. If prices for the necessities of life were to be raised drastically by the half-dozen family-owned enterprises that dominate Argentina's industries, there could be worker strikes and attempted military takeovers of the government, as in the past. People fear that inflation might return, too. Also of concern is the cattle industry, which built the nation and is doing poorly.

Argentina has a wealth of fertile land and talented people. Many hope that these two assets can stop the slide back to the political and economic troubles of the past. The challenge, they believe, will be to improve the lives of all Argentines—rich, poor, and middle class.

THE INVENTIVE ARGENTINES

Finding a typical Argentine is not easy because the nation's people come from many different backgrounds. In fact, this variety of backgrounds has probably led to one of their basic beliefs, respect for the individual. During the nineteenth century, Argentina's immigrants settled into largely German, Polish, Italian, Irish, or Jewish neighborhoods with little friction, even though the neighborhood next door might be different. Argentines believed in allowing individuals to be who they were, and the same holds true today.

Another clue to Argentines' basic beliefs is that nine out of ten people in the nation belong to the Roman Catholic Church. Although not everyone attends church services, many Argentines accept their church's teachings, including respect for the family and belief in God.

The Gaucho Tradition

Certain traits in today's Argentines might be traced to the gauchos of past centuries. By rounding up wild cattle for meat and leather and herding them to market, the gauchos made it possible for Argentina to draw wealth

from the Pampa. Most gauchos were mestizos who led hard and lonely lives away from the control of towns, the government, or the Church. Today, Argentines admire the independence and self-reliance shown by the gauchos—even though, at times, gauchos lived outside the law.

A popular expression says that to understand Argentina, you have to understand the gaucho. The gaucho was similar to the American cowboy, but his clothes were different. He wore a fringed poncho, a square of cloth with a hole for his head, and *bombachas*, or baggy pants, with a silver-ornamented belt at his waist and a wide strip of cloth between his legs. For a boot, he used the hide from the hind leg of a freshly killed colt, pulling it over his own foot and leg to dry in a boot shape. To his boots he fastened cruel-looking spurs. The spurs and a long knife hanging at his side were used to cut ropes and remove hides from cattle. His weapon was the *boleadoras*, made of stones bound with leather strips, which he threw at the legs of cattle and other animals to trip them.

The gaucho was a skilled rider, and he spent most of his day on horseback. Meat cut from the warm carcass of a wild cow and eaten raw was often his only food, and his drink was *mate*—a strong herbal tea served in a gourd and sipped through a silver straw called a *bombilla*. The gaucho's home—when he was there—was a mud hut covered with cowhides and containing little to sit on except

A modern-day gaucho, dressed for a parade. His flat black hat and the silver ornaments on his saddle are typical of Argentina's gauchos.

a few horse skulls for stools. Often he didn't marry the
woman he lived with, yet she raised his family, cooked his
food, milked the cows, made cheese, and wove raw wool
into warmth-giving ponchos.

Gauchos usually worked as cattle herders for a *patrón*,
a wealthy landowner. They also pledged to fight as soldiers
against the patrón's enemies if it became necessary—and
it often did.

Argentina's stories and songs celebrate the gaucho
figure above any other. In Buenos Aires, a popular
museum displays woven ponchos, belts decorated with
silver, bridle bits, and other mementos of gaucho life.
Martín Fierro, a 6,000-line poem written in 1872 by José
Hernández, is still studied by schoolchildren today. It tells
the story of one gaucho's struggle to save his way of life in
the wake of incoming settlers and the farms and fences
they brought.

The Gaucho Spirit Today

In today's Argentina, there is strong support for unions
and political parties, and this fierce loyalty reflects the
gaucho spirit. When the Pampa was fenced in during the
late nineteenth century, the frontier lifestyle began to
change, and many gauchos moved to the cities and became
working-class people. Because they no longer had patróns

to support, these workers gave their loyalty to unions and political parties.

Argentina's rural citizens probably admire the gaucho tradition more than city dwellers do. Like the gauchos, people in the country have closer ties to the land, and they tend to be very independent, relying on their families for help rather than on outsiders such as organizations or the government. Rural Argentines, like the gauchos, may depend on animals for income or even transportation. Livestock shows, markets, and horse races provide meeting places for farmers and ranchers who sometimes live far from their nearest neighbors.

Yet Argentines in the cities display another gaucho trait, stamina. Using sheer physical endurance, gauchos rode for hours, sometimes days, at a time; today life as it is lived in Argentina's cities calls for stamina, too. Porteños regularly work from about 9:00 A.M. until 7:00 P.M., with a long lunch hour. They think of 7:00 P.M. as late afternoon rather than evening. Dinner is served very late and can take two or more hours to complete. At night, people crowd Buenos Aires's streets, dining at restaurants, going to movie theaters, windowshopping, and sometimes returning home as late as 3:00 A.M.—even when the next day is a workday!

Argentines throughout the country respect another trait of the gauchos, courage. "We'll never be afraid again" is a line from a popular song that urged people to be brave as the country changed from its military government to a democracy. Argentina is famous for its international award-winning films; *The Official Story*, considered a classic, won an Oscar for best foreign film of the year in 1985. It tells the story of a woman who discovers that her adopted child had been born to a girl kidnapped by the military. The woman must face this difficult truth and find courage within herself.

Creative Solutions

Another trait that Argentines admire is inventiveness. Inventive behavior that solves problems has been demonstrated by Argentine individuals, business owners, and even whole cities. The story of Mendoza is a good example. Mendoza, a city on the dry eastern slopes of the Andes Mountains, has been destroyed by earthquakes many times in its past. To help their city survive, residents planted trees with very deep roots, built homes low to the earth, and made the streets wide. The many city parks provide a place for people to seek shelter if buildings crumble. This inventive and farsighted planning makes Mendoza safer when the frequent earthquakes shake the ground.

A wide, tree-lined street in the city of Mendoza.

Inventiveness is also shown in the way Argentine tea growers market their tea abroad. Although India and China are better known for their tea than Argentina, the country has become the biggest single exporter of black tea to the United States. Argentines learned that North Americans drink iced tea year-round in huge quantities, and they developed a special blend of tea for iced tea mixes. This inventive solution allowed Argentina to become part of the "international tea party."

Individuals in Argentina are also creative in solving problems. In Buenos Aires, a tangle of telephone lines hangs high over some streets. Because it can take a long time to get telephone service installed in homes and offices, some Argentines—tired of waiting—have put up telephone lines themselves, as a way of handling the problem of slow public service.

Books and Conversations

Argentina is a nation of enthusiastic readers. The large middle class takes pride in being well-read, and they buy a wide variety of magazines, newspapers, and books. World-famous literature is available in Spanish translations in bookstores. Children are often told, *"Libro cerrado no saca letrado,"* or "You don't learn anything from a closed book." Anyone who can read and discuss classic books intelligently is respected.

Buenos Aires alone has more than a thousand bookstores and a dozen major daily newspapers, including two in German, two in French, one in English, and one in Yiddish. The major English-language newspaper is the *Buenos Aires Herald*, known for its courageous coverage of human rights violations committed by the military governments. *Clarín* (Bugle), *La Prensa* (The Press), and *La Nación* (The Nation) are three Spanish-language newspapers recognized around the world for their quality.

A newsstand in Buenos Aires displays many of the magazines and newspapers that Argentines enjoy reading.

Argentines enjoy reading about and discussing almost any subject. When two Argentines meet, they usually greet each other with a pat on the back, a handshake, or a kiss for close friends, and then they begin a conversation. Throughout the country, Argentines can be seen talking over meals, over mate, or over tiny cups of strong black espresso coffee. Sidewalk cafes are full of customers having passionate discussions and friendly "arguments." Although the conversation may sometimes get loud, it's just the sound of ideas being shared!

National Dance

The Argentine national dance is the tango, a dance born a hundred years ago in Buenos Aires's waterfront district, where gauchos and dockworkers danced with women in gaucho saloons, or *pulperías*. Couples dancing the tango made sudden shifts and turns, gliding and dipping, keeping their knees sharply bent. The music was sad, a mixture of throbbing Spanish songs and French folk music that told the story of day-to-day life in the slums. One famous tango singer, Carlos Gardel, who was born about 1881, recorded songs for the radio and starred in early motion pictures.

Today in Argentina, *tango* means music as well as dance. At tango clubs in Buenos Aires, Argentines sip coffee or wine and watch as women and men sing tango, songs of suffering over lost love, while the *bandoneón,* a type of accordion, is played.

Folklore shows with music and dance from Argentina's wild west past are popular throughout the country. The *zamba*, danced with handkerchiefs flashing in the hands, is accompanied by lilting Andean pipe music from the Jujuy region. In the northwestern provinces, people dance the *carnavalito*, a centuries-old Indian dance. The gaucho folk dance *escondido*—a favorite at folklore shows—tells the story of a gaucho who must hide from real or imagined enemies.

Opera and an Eerie Museum

During opera season, men and women in formal dress crowd the *Teatro Colón* (Colon Theater) in Buenos Aires. Argentines love opera second only to tango. The Teatro Colón, which covers almost an entire city block, is one of the best-known opera houses in the world. Its stage can hold six hundred performers, an orchestra, and a company of ballet dancers.

Buenos Aires also has many revue theaters, where comics sometimes mock politics and political figures. At Teatro San Martín (Saint Martin Theater), a new city theater complex, performances featuring puppets, mimes, or dancers are popular. Cafe concerts, which have a single singer, comedian, or dancer performing, are held throughout the city in cellars.

Argentina, with more than 300 museums, is a museum-lover's paradise. In Buenos Aires, the eerie Penitentiary Museum is located in a mournful former prison. Nearby, the Museum of Telecommunications is a fantasy land where carved gnomes peer from walls and visitors learn the history of the telephone and information about computers and fax machines.

The Man Who Saw Imaginary Beings

In his later years, Jorge Luis Borges could not see the

faces of people he met or tell the color of their hair. He had gone slowly blind as had his great-grandfather, grandfather, and father. Yet Borges could describe people and scenes so colorfully in his writing that he has become Argentina's most beloved poet and story writer. Borges lived from 1899 until 1986 and was twice nominated for a Nobel prize for literature. Today he is one of the most widely read writers in all of Latin America.

Like other Latin American writers, Borges felt driven to write about his country's politics. After he wrote articles critical of those in power, government agents attended the classes he taught at the University of Buenos Aires to monitor what he was saying. To Borges, they were spies. He always had a sense of humor, though. As a young man, he was fired from a library job for his politics, and he liked to tell people that he had been named, instead, to the lowly post of poultry inspector.

Borges is loved by Argentines because, in speaking his opinion, he displayed the courage they respect. Argentines also admire his independence and inventiveness, two qualities that shape their own daily lives and the life of their country. The citizens of Argentina are a well-read people who enjoy sharing ideas and value the ability to communicate. These qualities, many Argentines believe, could help solve their nation's political and economic problems.

FROM SILVER TO WHEAT

For hundreds of years, more than two dozen Indian tribes roamed the mountain valleys, deserts, jungles, and grasslands of Argentina. Some were nomadic hunters, while others farmed. In the flat Pampa, tribes such as the Querandí hunted by running down small deer on foot and flinging *boleadoras* at their legs to trip them. Indians in the Guaraní tribe of the northern Paraná River were farmers who grew squash, melons, and sweet potatoes in jungle clearings.

In 1516 the first Europeans to reach Argentina sailed into the Río de la Plata. The expedition was seeking a route around the southern tip of South America to the Pacific Ocean. It did not fare well. The leader, a Spanish navigator named Juan Díaz de Solís, was killed and eaten by Indians who had seemed friendly. Survivors of this ill-fated journey returned to Spain as quickly as they could. A later expedition led by Sebastian Cabot found friendlier Indians and traded with them for silver, which was brought back to Spain. These few pieces of silver fired enthusiasm in Europe to search for silver near the Río de la Plata.

Ferdinand Magellan, a Portuguese navigator sailing under the flag of Spain, entered the mouth of the Río de la Plata in 1520. Because he had heard the stories about Solís, he wisely did not explore the river's shores. Instead, he sailed farther south along the Argentine coast and discovered the Strait of Magellan, which bears his name today.

Settlers, Missionaries, and Smugglers

In 1536, Pedro de Mendoza, a Spanish nobleman, built a fort on the banks of the Río de la Plata, naming it *Buenos Aires* ("good airs") after an Italian patron saint, Our Lady of Saint Mary of the Good Airs. This first Buenos Aires failed. Promised supply ships didn't arrive, and the starving settlers ate snakes, horsehides, and even rats. Angered by European settlement on their lands, Querandí Indians raided the fort, burning the straw roofs of the sod huts. The colonists finally abandoned the fort and moved hundreds of miles upriver to found Asunción, today the capital of Paraguay. Fifty years later, settlers from Asunción returned to build a second Buenos Aires. It succeeded, but no silver was ever found near the Río de la Plata.

The first permanent settlements in Argentina were established in the northwestern part of the country by Spanish colonists following the old Inca roads from Peru. For almost 200 years, northern Argentina was the focus of Spanish attention. In the sixteenth century, Jesuit

Ruins of the sixteenth-century Jesuit missions in northern Argentina

missionaries from Spain gathered the peaceful Guaraní Indians into settlements on the upper Paraná River, converting them to the Roman Catholic religion. The Guaraní learned to weave cotton cloth, tan hides into leather, construct boats, work with wood, and make musical instruments. The communities exported yerba mate, cotton, and tobacco, and were so successful that nearby landowners objected to their prosperity. A decree issued by the Spanish crown in 1767 forced the Jesuits to leave Argentina. Some Guaraní were sold as slaves, but others returned to the jungle.

Because Spain considered Argentina's coast a hostile land without wealth and the home of dangerous Indians, the Spanish rulers did not allow goods to land there. Instead, goods were shipped thousands of miles overland by mule from Spanish settlements on the north coast of the continent. Córdoba, Tucumán, Salta, and other Argentine cities on this overland trade route grew prosperous while Buenos Aires, a city of about 20,000 by 1750, and the coast were neglected.

The resourceful porteños found their own way to trade—smuggling. Ships carrying illegal goods hid in the many winding river branches where the Spanish authorities could not find them. African slaves, ironware, cloth, and sugar all entered the city by this forbidden route. Buenos Aires's economy flourished from sales of smuggled goods. Finally in 1776, Spain combined all its colonies in southeastern South America into the Viceroyalty of the Río de la Plata. Buenos Aires was the capital, and for the first time ships were allowed to dock and unload goods along the Argentine coast.

By 1800, Buenos Aires had 40,000 inhabitants. As it increased in size and importance, it tried to control the entire country politically. The inland provinces had been the economic center of the region for 200 years, and they resisted the effort. Soon a power struggle developed between growing Buenos Aires and the established interior provinces.

The Struggle for Independence

In 1806, Buenos Aires was attacked by a British fleet determined to win a colony for Britain in South America. The Spanish, taken by surprise, did not defend the city against the invading troops, and a citizen army of porteños quickly assembled and defeated the British. The victory inspired confidence; the citizens overthrew the Spanish officials in the city, replacing them with local people. When the British tried to invade Buenos Aires again in 1807, they were soundly beaten a second time by the self-confident porteños.

On May 25, 1810, leaders in Buenos Aires formed their own independent government, but this was only the beginning of Argentina's movement toward total independence. Porteños had tasted freedom from Spanish rule, but many people in the interior were still loyal to Spain. This deepened the split between Buenos Aires and the interior and led to a confusing period when the fate of Argentina seemed uncertain.

General José de San Martín, called the George Washington of Argentina, broke the hold that Spain had on

General José de San Martín

Argentina. He helped persuade the interior provinces to declare Argentina's independence at the Congress of Tucumán on July 9, 1816. San Martín believed that, for Argentina to be completely free, Spain had to be driven from the entire South American continent. To achieve this, he secretly trained volunteers into a small, expert fighting force. In 1817, his troops crossed the Andes Mountains and defeated the Spanish fortress in Chile and, later, Peru. In northern Argentina, near Salta, General Martín Miguel de Güemes assisted the fight for freedom by leading armies of gauchos against Spanish invaders from the north.

A Troubled Freedom

The new nation was called United Provinces of the Río de la Plata. It was torn by civil war between *unitarios*, who wanted a strong central government with its headquarters in Buenos Aires, and *federales*, who wanted to keep the provinces independent.

In 1829, Juan Manuel de Rosas was elected governor of Buenos Aires. Over time, he became the nation's dictator. He was a *federale* landowner who had made money by threatening and murdering others. Red was the official color of his government, and landowners were careful to wear red ponchos to show their loyalty. Rosas used spies and secret police, and exhibited the heads of his assassinated enemies in public. He was finally forced out of office in 1852. Unfortunately, Argentines had become accustomed to the secret police and terrorism Rosas used, and this started a long-lasting trend for the country.

Using the U.S. Constitution as a model, Argentina adopted a national constitution in 1853. Buenos Aires refused to accept this constitution and remained independent for several years before rejoining the rest of the nation. With a few changes, the same constitution is still in use today. One important clause allows the president to assume certain powers in an emergency. This clause in the constitution has been used many times by Argentina's presidents.

A Booming Economy

In northern Argentina, Spanish and Indian peoples lived peacefully together, and marriages between the two groups were common. To the south, it was different. Small, fast-moving bands of Indians on wild horses raided towns, plundering and burning. From 1878 to 1883, wars flared between the settlers and the Indians. Government troops and gaucho armies led by landowners tracked the Indians' movements with the telegraph and then used the repeating rifle to defeat them. By the end of these wars, most Indians of the Pampa and northern Patagonia had been killed.

After a century of fighting and dictatorship, Argentina now prospered. Railroads across the plains made trade and travel easier. Nearly a million immigrants arrived between 1880 and 1889, mostly from Italy and Spain. British immigrants invested money in the meat-packing and banking industries, strengthening Argentina's economy and making it a power in world trade.

The Pampa had been divided into estates as large as 100,000 acres and awarded mainly to people who had aided in the Indian Wars. Land meant wealth and power for estate owners, but most rural Argentines were poor. Immigrants farmed small plots of an estate, sharing the income from crops with the owner. As the vast estates were fenced in, fewer gauchos were needed to control cattle herds. Those without work moved to city slums to take low-paying jobs. Fences ended a way of life for most gauchos.

Times remained good economically for Argentina during the next decades. Reforms were passed, workers were given a minimum wage, and businesses prospered. In 1929, the world economy crumbled, and so did Argentina's. People lost money they had deposited in banks. Runaway inflation ruined businesses. With less foreign demand for Argentina's beef and grain exports, the country was forced to establish an income tax. The Great Depression also affected Argentina's politics, launching a series of military governments and dictators that lasted to the early 1980s.

World War II caused great divisions in Argentina. Many Argentines of Italian or German origin favored the Axis countries of Germany, Italy, and Japan. Other Argentines wanted ties to Britain, the United States, and the Allies. Argentina declared itself neutral, but at the war's end in 1945, it entered the war on the Allies' side, never having fought in battle.

The Peróns in Power

Juan Domingo Perón, a young military officer, became president of Argentina in 1946. He knew that the Argentine

Eva Duarte de Perón and President Juan Perón

working class felt neglected by those in power, and he helped organize these workers into unions, raised their wages, and built houses for them. Under his leadership, women were given the right to vote. In this way, Perón became a hero to the *descamisados*, or "shirtless ones," as he called the working class. Yet Perón was also a dictator who used secret police, terrorism, and strong-arm tactics.

For nine years, Perón remained in power. His popularity was strengthened by the help of his second wife, Eva Duarte de Perón, who was immensely popular with

the workers. She started the Eva Duarte de Perón
Foundation, which gave money to the poor. In return, the
workers held demonstrations of affection for Evita, as they
called her. When she died of cancer in 1952, enormous
crowds in city plazas carried candles to mourn her death.

Perón began losing control of his followers,
the *Peronistas*, after Eva's death. He punished anyone
he felt was guilty of treason, limited free speech and
the actions of political parties, censored the press,
and even threw some of his supporters out of office.
Over time, he lost most of his popularity. In 1955 military
planes bombed the presidential palace while troops
attacked from the street. Perón survived the revolt, but a
few months later the military tried again and succeeded.
Perón fled to Spain. In 1973 he returned to Argentina and
was elected president again, but he became ill and died a
year later.

Perón's third wife, Isabel Martínez de Perón, had
been his vice-president. When he died, she became
president, the first woman to be chief of state in any North
or South American country. With little experience as
a leader, she faced her country's many problems—a failing
economy, a soaring inflation rate, and terrorism. She was
unable to solve these problems, and the military leaders
again took over Argentina's government in March 1976.

The Dirty Wars

In the late 1970s and early 1980s, the Argentine people held violent demonstrations against the military government, soaring inflation, and unemployment. The military *junta*, or generals in control, fought these demonstrators with violence of their own, and their campaign of repression became known as the dirty wars. Men, women, and even children were kidnapped and secretly tortured by the military, never to be seen again. They became known as *los desaparecidos*, the "missing." Argentines were afraid for their own safety and that of their families, and most were careful not to say anything that might draw the attention of the government.

About 15,000 Argentines disappeared during this time, including many who were innocent. One group of Argentines is especially admired for their bravery during the dirty wars. The Mothers of the Plaza de Mayo marched every Thursday in the plaza across from the presidential palace, demanding that the government tell them what happened to their missing family members.

In 1982, the junta, perhaps searching for an issue to take people's minds off the failing economy and the dirty wars, drew international attention to a small group of islands off the country's southern Atlantic coast. Argentina has long claimed these islands and calls them *Las Islas Malvinas*. Great Britain names these same islands the

Falklands and has also laid claim to them since 1833.

Led by General Leopoldo Galtieri, the junta ordered Argentine troops to invade the Malvinas Islands, but England took the windswept islands back in a fierce ten-week battle. During this time, Argentine airplanes destroyed a number of English ships, and exploding ammunition lit the skies over the once-peaceful islands where sheep had grazed. Almost 1,100 Argentines lost their lives, and Argentina lost the war.

Losing disgraced the military government. Military officers were ashamed to be seen in their uniforms on the streets because they had lost the people's support. In 1983, elections were held to return control of the government from the military to the citizens, and Argentina became a democracy.

A Return to Democracy

Raúl Alfonsín, an outspoken lawyer, was elected president of Argentina in 1983. He assured Argentines that he would restore human rights, and his first act as president was to try to learn what had happened to los desaparecidos. He even put the terrorist leaders on trial, including military officers and officials from the last Peronista government. Several military leaders were found guilty of violating human rights and sent to prison.

At first, a surge of enthusiasm for the new democracy shook Argentina. Soon, though, problems began to surface as inflation rose dramatically. Food, housing, and clothing cost many times more than in 1982, the year before, but the people earned less than in 1970. The economy was like a time bomb because its problems refused to go away. The debt Argentina owed to other countries grew to $56 billion by the end of the 1980s, and interest payments alone were $4 billion.

In 1989, Carlos Saúl Menem, a Peronista, was elected president of Argentina. He faced serious problems, especially the continuing dramatic rise in the cost of living. To help poor Argentines afford life's necessities, President Menem hammered out economic reforms, which met with amazing success. Within five years, inflation was reduced from 5,000 percent to 7 percent! The economy was stronger, too. In 1995, Menem won reelection by vowing to smash another foe—unemployment.

Some Argentines believe that the continued success of their democracy may be determined by the health of their country's economy. Whether Argentina's democracy flourishes might depend on whether people are able to find adequate homes and an acceptable standard of living, Argentina has had five free elections in a row, the most it has had in over 60 years. This is a hopeful sign.

BIRD STORIES AND MONSTER LEGENDS

Stories and legends from Argentina often feature two subjects, monsters and birds. The monster tales usually come from Patagonia, but bird stories are told in all parts of the country. Argentines describe birds in a colorful and affectionate way—the ostrich-like rheas are called dusty clouds of the Pampa because of their habit of snuggling into loose dirt and shaking their feathers. Argentines tell legends about rheas, flamingos, doves, pigeons, humming-birds, and songbirds.

Salta, in northern Argentina, is called the Province of Legends. One of the most famous legends tells why a bird called the crespin has a sad song, why a winged insect called the cicada drones on loudly, and why the two are often heard together. There are many versions of this story, but this one is told frequently.

Crespin

Once there were two handsome young men named Coyuyo and Crespin. Both lived in the north, but their homes were in different territories. Coyuyo grew up in a warm and happy home with a good family and good

A clay statue of a parrot, made by early Argentine Indians. Argentines have long been fascinated with birds.

friends. He had been given a gift—a wonderful voice with which to sing the songs of his people. When he sang, the sound was so beautiful that everyone stopped to listen. People came from miles away to hear Coyuyo strum his guitar and sing folk songs, and soon they began to say, "Not only is Coyuyo the best singer in town, he is the most wonderful singer anywhere."

In a territory not very far away lived Crespin. He too had been blessed with a special singing voice, and he too played the guitar and sang the tunes of his homeland. His family, friends, and neighbors begged over and over to hear Crespin sing for them; he was often asked to sing at fiestas and celebrations. When someone was sick, Crespin soothed away the illness with gentle songs. People from the far reaches of the territory heard about Crespin and came to listen for themselves. They began to say, "Not only is Crespin the best singer in town, he is the most wonderful singer on earth."

Soon, each territory claimed to have the best singer. People began to argue back and forth. "Our Coyuyo is better!" "No! Our Crespin makes him sound like a donkey!"

It was decided to hold a contest to determine who was the best singer in the north. On the chosen day, people from both territories gathered to listen to their heroes perform. Those for Crespin were sure he would win; those who favored Coyuyo were confident he would make his opponent sound like a beginner. They crowded around the town square, eagerly waiting for the contest to begin.

Coyuyo sang first. When he finished, his supporters cheered and applauded and waved handkerchiefs in salute. Then Crespin took up his guitar. His voice rose with the words of a story-song. The audience grew quiet to listen. Women began to cry softly at the beauty of the melody, strong men were moved by the song's message as sung in Crespin's clear voice, and crying babies were lulled to innocent sleep. When Crespin finished and put aside his guitar, there was an unearthly silence. No one could speak. Finally a great cheer arose. It was clear that Crespin had won. Coyuyo hid his bitter disappointment and congratulated Crespin.

"You have won," he said, shaking his opponent's hand. He drank a toast to Crespin's victory, and the two rode off together. Once they were out of everyone's sight in the forest, Coyuyo killed Crespin and buried him.

Crespin's frightened horse ran off and went home. Seeing the horse without its master, Crespin's wife knew immediately that something bad had happened, and she went in search of her husband. Desperate, she wandered around and around in the dense forest, calling out his name in anguish. Finally she turned into a small bird whose song had a deep note of suffering, crying over and over, "Crespin! Crespin!"

Coyuyo could not bear the sadness in the bird's cry because it reminded him of his crime. Haunted and maddened by the sound, he buried himself in the ground and turned into a cicada. But Heaven punished him, and at certain times of the year he must leave his underground prison and go aboveground, where once again he hears the haunting song of the crespin. The cicada attempts to drown out this terrible sound by raising his voice to cover the song of the bird that tortures him.

The Land of Monsters

Many Argentine legends—ancient Indian myths, tales from the first European explorers, and more recent stories of folk heroes—come from the wild, windswept steppes of Patagonia. For centuries, people believed that Patagonia was a land of monsters, giants with big feet, and other "beasties." Even in this century, expeditions journeyed to Patagonia in the hope of finding live dinosaurs!

Early in the twentieth century, two bandits from the United States named Butch Cassidy and the Sundance Kid heard stories of this wild place called Patagonia. When U.S. marshals came close to catching them, they robbed a bank of $30,000 and sailed to Buenos Aires. They asked the Argentine officials if there were outlaws in Patagonia, and were glad to be told there were none— they wanted to be the only outlaws operating there.

Today, Patagonians still tell stories about these *bandoleros norteamericanos*, or North American outlaws. Some Patagonians insist that their fathers or grandfathers knew the bandits personally and that Butch and Sundance were not bad men, but folk heroes.

One tale tells how the pair tricked a Patagonian village by dressing as "real" wild west robbers and galloping up and down the streets on horseback, firing guns into the air and putting on a western show. The unsuspecting villagers cheered the outlaws' wild antics and laughed at *los gringos locos*, the crazy foreigners. When an unsuspecting banker invited the bandits to lunch, Butch and Sundance suddenly stopped pretending and tied the poor man up, stuffing all the bank's money into a bag. Outside the bank, the villagers—none the wiser—waved at the pair, who tipped their hats and waved back as they rode calmly out of sight.

The Old Chief and the *Caudillo*

Argentina's wild west stories resemble stories told in the United States, except that Argentine "cowboy-Indian" tales center on the conflict between the Indians and the *caudillos*, or rich landowners, with their bands of gauchos. During the nineteenth century, both sides fought to control Argentina's rich lands. In stories such as this one, one side often outsmarts the other.

An elderly Indian chief found great pleasure in hunting and fishing with his grandson. The old man and the boy always rode together on a white horse. One day, as the two rode through a mountain valley, they were surprised by a caudillo and his band of gauchos and were taken prisoner. Their hands were bound with leather strips, and they were tied to a tree.

Argentina's wild west history is the source of many legends and stories.

That night, while the gauchos and caudillo slept, the Indian chief freed himself and his grandson, and the two slipped quietly past their sleeping enemies to the horses. The old man mounted his white horse, lifted the boy up with him, and, hanging low along the horse's side to avoid the gauchos' bullets, the pair disappeared into the night.

The caudillo was furious that an old man and a child could escape him so easily. When his gauchos prepared to chase the two, the caudillo stopped them, shouting that he could recapture an old man and a boy without help. He took food and a string of his best horses, and followed them. Yet, try as he might, he couldn't catch the white horse with its riders. The old Indian chief and his grandson escaped unharmed, but the caudillo—whose pride was wounded—could not forget and never stopped searching for the old chief and the small boy.

The Legend of Luján

Forty miles (64 kilometers) west of Buenos Aires a beautiful Roman Catholic cathedral is built on the spot where a legend began. Occasionally, people walk the entire distance from Buenos Aires to this church to show their belief in the legend, which tells how a traveler received a message to build the church where it sits today. Here is one version of the legend of Luján.

Three hundred years ago, a weary traveler slowly made his way to the banks of the Luján River with his belongings and a clay statue of the Virgin Mary in the back of his wooden oxcart. The man urged his oxen forward into the river, but the wheels of the heavy cart bogged down in the thick mud, catching fast.

The traveler—wise in the ways of crossing rivers—soon found a long stick and dry grasses, and used them to free the cart. As soon as the wheels were out of the mud, the traveler commanded his oxen to move forward, but when they did, something fell from the back of the cart with a thud. Walking behind the cart, the traveler found his statue of the Virgin lying unbroken on the muddy ground. He lifted the statue and returned it safely to the cart, but when he tried again to cross the river, the oxen refused to move. The man shouted loudly at the animals, urging them ahead in every way he knew. Yet no matter what he did, the beasts would not budge.

Finally, in desperation, the traveler took the statue from his cart and set it on the ground. Only then would the oxen walk ahead. The traveler built a small shrine around the statue of the Virgin and went on his way. Today, the basilica of Luján sits on that same spot.

The Poncho

Some colorful Argentine sayings revolve around the poncho that gauchos wore. The poncho, worn like a coat, served many purposes for its wearer. It warmed him as he slept, protected him against wind and rain, and shielded him from knife wounds when he wrapped it around his forearm during a fight. The color of a poncho told where its owner lived—black and white ponchos came from the Pampa, while blood-red and multicolored ones were from the north. Women wore ponchos too,

fastening them on one shoulder. It should not be surprising that Argentines have expressions about something which was as important as the poncho was to its owner.

If an Argentine tells you that you have "stepped on your poncho," it means you have made a mistake. An Argentine who is suspicious of someone else might say, "I wonder what he has under his poncho." It is the same as saying, "I wonder what he has up his sleeve," and means that the speaker doesn't trust the other person.

According to a proverb, there are ponchos for everyone. Rich people warm themselves with fine ponchos woven of sheep's wool or the soft fleece from llama-like vicuñas or gaunacos. For the poor, there is warmth from another kind of poncho—"Sunlight is the poncho of the poor," the proverb says very simply.

These sayings about ponchos have been passed down by generations of Argentines as part of a colorful tradition of storytelling. Like many Argentine stories, legends, and sayings, they explain an aspect of nature or everyday life, or allow the listener to escape the ordinary world and go on an imaginary adventure.

Ponchos are still worn by some rural Argentines, such as this man in the mountains near Jujuy.

FIESTAS AND HOLIDAYS

The people of different backgrounds who settled Argentina brought their cherished holiday traditions with them. Native Argentine Indians also had colorful festivals of their own. Today, Argentines celebrate dozens of different holidays—patriotic and religious days, festivals honoring the earth and their gaucho heritage, and an exciting party called Carnival. Some of these holidays are celebrated everywhere in Argentina, but many of them take place in only one region of the country or, at times, in only a single village.

Carnival and Easter Celebration

About six weeks before Easter, Carnival is celebrated in many parts of Argentina. It is an opportunity to have fun before Lent, when Christians begin to observe the solemn time of preparation for Easter. Carnival occurs at the beginning of Argentina's fall, when the weather is still warm. In some ways, it is like Labor Day in the United States—a last chance to have a summer picnic or party before school starts and people return to the daily routine.

During Carnival, people dress up in costumes to look like clowns, animals, cartoon characters—anything grand

Most Argentines are Roman Catholics, and they celebrate many religious holidays. Here, a procession carries a cross decorated with colorful flowers.

or silly that is different from everyday life. Some
children's costumes at Carnival, such as kings and queens,
witches and fairy princesses, are also favorites with
children in the United States at Halloween. Young people
sometimes plan their elaborate costumes a whole year
ahead of time!

During the evening, oversized hats, shoes, and masks
stand out as merrymakers parade down plazas and streets.
Traditionally the marchers carry sweet basil, the scented
flower of the Carnival, and signs with caricatures, or
cartoon drawings, of well-known local people.
Occasionally these cartoons have a political message, but
usually it's all done in good fun.

Carnival is a more important festival in northwestern
Argentina than elsewhere in the country. Cerrillos, Cafayate,
San Carlos, Salta, and other cities still celebrate Carnival
the way it was done a century ago. Salta has the biggest
celebration of all. The people of Salta hang colorful
decorations, and children dress as Indians, wearing large
masks decorated with bits of mirror, feathers, and glass eyes.
Inside brightly colored tents, people dance the zamba and
eat spicy food such as corn stew or corn patties wrapped and
cooked in the husks.

The best advice anyone can get during Carnival is,
"Watch out for water balloons!" All Argentine carnivals,
no matter where in the country, feature surprise water

balloon attacks. Boys throw them at girls, and girls throw them at boys. Children even wait on rooftops, hoping to dampen the clothes of someone walking by. People often end up going home to change clothes several times, but no one minds because it's all part of Carnival.

Carnival ends as Lent begins. The last week of Lent is called Holy Week, and many Argentines attend church during these days, which include Good Friday and Easter. Good Friday is a sad and serious public holiday, but Easter is a happy celebration. Argentines eat seafood more frequently during Lent, and mothers or grandmothers might bake *empanadas*, little pies that are specially stuffed with fish or vegetables for Easter. Another tradition is a cake in the shape of a ring, but what boys and girls look forward to most are big chocolate Easter eggs with tiny candies hidden inside.

Christmas in Argentina

In Argentina, Christmas is celebrated on December 25, the same as in North America, but in Argentina this is summertime, not winter. Shortly before Christmas, people shop for presents and mail Christmas cards. Most homes have a Christmas tree—often an artificial one—that is decorated with lights, delicate glass balls, different colors of ribbon, and little figures of favorite animals. Families

A Christmas tree in an Argentine home

usually trim the tree together. In some homes, a miniature nativity scene, showing the birth of Jesus, is displayed in a windowsill or on a cloth-covered table.

Christmas Eve is sometimes a bigger celebration than Christmas Day. On Christmas Eve, grandparents, uncles, aunts, and cousins may arrive, bringing wrapped gifts and hugs and kisses. A special meal—often cold beef, chicken, or turkey, and fruit salad—is eaten later, perhaps as late as 11:30 P.M.. Because the weather is warm, families sometimes have their feast outside on decorated tables.

After the dinner, traditional plates of almonds and

dried fruits are set out, along with another favorite—
pan dulce, a sweet bread with fewer fruits and nuts than
fruitcake. When it is midnight, the gifts are opened.
Children might get toys or perhaps something new to wear.
Because it is a special night, bedtime can be as late as 1:00
A.M. On Christmas Day itself, Argentines usually stay
home; sometimes friends drop in with holiday greetings or
gifts of food.

January 6 is *Día de los Reyes,* or Day of the Kings.
It is also called Three Kings Day because it marks the visit
of the three wisemen to the baby Jesus. In some areas,
people dress up to look like the three kings and ride down
the streets on horses instead of the camels the kings rode.
The night before Three Kings Day, children put their shoes
outside or hide them somewhere in the house. The next
morning when they look, toys and gifts are sitting by their
shoes, left there by the three kings.

National Holidays

All of Argentina celebrates its national holidays. One
of the biggest celebrations is New Year's. In Buenos Aires,
New Year's Eve is marked by many noisy parades. Cars
and buses wrapped in colored banners travel parade routes
with much honking and noise. At midnight, *fuegos
artificiales*, or fireworks, explode in every direction.

Families, friends, and neighbors meet for parties and merrymaking at their homes or social clubs. Young people are allowed to stay up very late and throw confetti on people—no one could be expected to sleep as fireworks continue through the night.

Argentina has several national patriotic holidays, including Flag Day on June 20 and the anniversary of the death of General José de San Martín on August 17. On national holidays, banks and some businesses are closed, and patriotic speeches and parades draw crowds throughout the country. In Buenos Aires, holiday processions often begin in the historic Plaza de Mayo under a blaze of flags. Gala opera performances are held for the anniversary of the Revolution of 1810 on May 25 and for Independence Day on July 9. Politicians and influential people attend these performances, dressed in formal clothing.

In Argentina, each kind of worker—postal employees, dockworkers, airline pilots, meat packers, and others—has its own union. On May 1, Labor Day, union members march in parades, carrying banners and signs bearing the symbol of their union. Family and friends stand along the parade route, taking photos, waving, and showing support for the union. Afterward, the unions host parties and celebrations for their members.

Festivals Honoring the Earth

Many cities and regions in Argentina sponsor festivals to honor aspects of nature that are important to the people. In July in Buenos Aires's Palermo Park, a livestock show and fiesta celebrate the importance of Argentina's cattle industry to the country's economy. Among those attending is the Argentine president, who traditionally wears a black tuxedo for the occasion and sits in a special box in the stands. During the show, Argentina's finest bulls—who have been washed, dried, groomed, and had their hooves manicured—are paraded around a ring, and the champion shorthorn bull of the year is chosen. This champion bull becomes the symbol for the important cattle industry, and he is given a fitting title of respect and dignity, Mr. Bull. A few lucky children are picked to have their photograph taken with Mr. Bull, who, as the fiesta's star, has his harness covered with championship ribbons.

The Andean city of San Carlos de Bariloche, or Bariloche, holds its Snow Festival during the winter month of August. International skiing competitions take place on the white mountains outside of town, which ring with the shouts of spectators watching the ski races. During a special ceremony, flags of the participating countries are honored; later, there are concerts, dances, a snowman-building contest for children, and the crowning of the Queen of Chocolate and the Queen of Snow. At night a torchlight procession winds its way down the mountain slopes. Recalling their Swiss heritage, the people of Bariloche serve traditional Swiss cakes and hot port wine spiced with cinnamon.

During grape harvest time in March, the people of Mendoza remember that their lives depend on the sun, rain, and the grapes that ripen from the earth. *La Fiesta de la Vendimia* is a three-day-long festival that celebrates the region's winemaking industry. First the ripe grapes are blessed on the vines, and then many carts filled with grapes are paraded through the streets, followed by crowds of young people on decorated bicycles. A queen is crowned in a special ceremony, and many of Mendoza's more than one thousand winemaking establishments serve free red wine. At least two thousand people are needed to present the festival's finish, fireworks with spectacular light and sound effects.

Not all earth festivals celebrate gifts from the land. Mar del Plata, Argentina's famous resort on the Atlantic coast, has a festival honoring the harvest taken from the rich fishing grounds just off its shores. Traditionally, people enjoy seafood banquets of shrimp, crab, and scallops. After the banquet, the Queen of the Sea, riding in a giant seashell, leads a parade of marchers who are dressed in sea-creature costumes.

Celebration of a Miracle

Over a hundred years ago, Welsh colonists first arrived on the isolated Patagonian shores and faced a winter of hardship and maddening winds. Because they came from a land with ample rain, they had no idea how to irrigate crops, and they nearly starved. Every July their descendants hold festivals called *Eisteddfods* to celebrate what is considered a miracle—the survival of their ancestors during that first terrible winter in Patagonia. Songs, plays, and poems tell the Welsh pioneers' story. The best ones win prizes. The celebration keeps alive the Welsh language, traditions, and music. Much-loved treats such as black cake are eaten at Welsh tea parties during this event.

Every year on September 15 the people of Salta relive the festival of Our Lord of the Miracle, a Roman Catholic celebration in remembrance of a miracle they believe happened in their province. In 1592 a statue of Jesus Christ washed up out of the sea and was carried inland to Salta. People declared that it had saved the city from frequent earthquakes and other dangers. To remember this miracle today, the people of Salta put on their best clothes and hold parades throughout the province. The statue of Christ is taken out of the Cathedral of Salta by a crowd of people who sing songs of faith as they carry it through the streets.

Gauchos ride in a traditional parade in San Antonio de Areco.

Black-Bordered Ponchos

The contributions of the gaucho, an Argentine folk hero, are the focus of celebrations in certain areas of the country. In Salta, gauchos of today recall the bravery of gauchos of the past. On June 16 they light fires by the city's monument to General Martín Miguel de Güemes, who led gaucho troops against Spanish forces during the war for independence. At night they sing songs that tell how the gaucho armies defended the liberty of Argentina. The anniversary of de Güemes's death on June 17 is honored with a parade of gauchos dressed in huge pairs of leather chaps and blackbordered ponchos of red or the color that represents the gaucho's town. The gauchos wear black scarves to mourn their lost leader, de Güemes.

A two-hour drive northwest of Buenos Aires lies the heart of gaucho country. For a week in November, the town of San Antonio de Areco revives the spirit of the independent gaucho of the last century. Residents dress as gauchos in black flat-crowned hats, baggy pants tucked into boots, and wide belts studded with silver coins. During this time ordinary people can pretend to be gauchos, heroes of the Pampa.

Some of Argentina's holidays and festivals are lighthearted, happy occasions. Others are serious expressions of religious faith. Still others give thanks for nature's bounty or mark a patriotic event from the past. All of these celebrations help give meaning and tradition to the daily lives of Argentines.

ARGENTINES EN CASA

During a busy workday, Argentines may use the expression *andar como bola sin manija*, which means they have spent the day "going around in circles" and not getting much done. Their evenings tend to be less hectic. The entire *familia*, or family, is often *en casa,* at home, relaxing, enjoying good food, watching television, and just talking with each other. At times, everyone seems to be doing all of this at once!

Many Kinds of Houses

There is really no typical Argentine house. Argentines may live in apartments, brick suburban homes, large mansions, small farmhouses, or rundown shacks in the slums. Some upper-class homes even look much like the historic villas and chalets found in the European country-side. Most Argentine homes, though, are made of brick. In the country, adobe is also common because it is inexpensive and warm. Wood and stone are used much less often because few trees grow on the pampas or in Patagonia, and the pampas do not have stone for building.

Argentine villages and cities are usually laid out around a tree-shaded plaza, a plan passed along by Spanish settlers,

A brick home of a well-to-do family in a suburb of Buenos Aires

who often built a fort in the town center. In smaller towns and suburbs, the streets are lined with single-family homes, often painted blue or green, favorite colors for houses. Some homes have sections with fresher-looking paint that are often newer than the rest of the house. Rather than moving to a larger house, many Argentines will build an addition to their home, sometimes even a new second story.

Some neighborhoods may have partly finished houses with piles of bricks or concrete blocks lying beside them or stored in sheds. These homes are not unwanted or abandoned. Because homeowners are afraid that prices will rise with inflation, they buy building materials as they can afford them. Sixty percent of Argentines own their homes, but they often build them in stages, adding rooms as needed.

Most Argentine homes have modern kitchens with indoor plumbing, but electricity is expensive and not often used. In many rural areas, natural gas heats homes, and small gas tanks are delivered by horse and cart. In smaller towns, vendors driving horse-carts knock on doors, hoping to sell vegetables, fruits, milk, or even baskets.

Tall apartment houses rise on most city skylines. Because the average Argentine family is smaller than families in other South American countries, apartments make ideal living quarters. There are modern, glass-fronted apartments for families with larger incomes, and older apartment buildings for those with less to spend on rent. An Argentine family can spend up to three-quarters of their monthly earnings on rent, and they must often sign a lease stating that they will live in the apartment for two years with agreed-to raises in the rent. Sometimes, people have to work at two jobs just to pay for rent and food.

Rural Argentines live in a variety of houses, from simple shacks for farm laborers to roomy farmhouses—frequently painted white, with red or brown roofs—which belong to the farm owner or manager. Wealthy landowners have built mansions on their *estancias,* or ranches, in the countryside, with swimming pools, tennis courts, and polo fields. The homes of rural poor people are called *ranchos*, and when their sons or daughters marry, they may simply build an addition onto their houses, around the central patio.

Around the Home

Certain things are commonly found in most Argentine households, whether they are modest or elaborate. Bicycles usually lean against a wall in most Argentine homes. Both girls and boys love riding bikes and spend hours practicing turns and racing friends, but

Argentines also use bikes as a convenient method of transportation. In some smaller towns, a father, mother, and one or two young children may all perch on a bike to run an errand or go to the movies.

Even though most Argentines own cars—usually compact cars—they often prefer to ride the *colectivo* (a system of brightly painted buses), subways, or trains. Unpaved country roads occasionally flood and make driving risky. In the city, traffic tie-ups are an increasing problem, and many drivers park their cars and ride subways to work. Special lanes in traffic-packed streets are used by people who ride in car pools.

In addition to a bicycle and a car, most Argentine homes probably have a pet. The best-loved pets are dogs or birds, such as singing canaries and parrots that are trained to talk. Country children might have horses as pets, and in Posadas, a town in the northeast, families keep pet sheep to graze on their grass and shrubs. In coastal Patagonia or on the pampas, a regular caller at dinnertime might be an armadillo, a hard-shelled animal that rolls into a ball when alarmed. Armadillos are shy, but their constant hunger makes it possible to feed them as pets.

In warm weather, Argentines like to open their windows and doors to catch the breeze. The background noise floating out of many homes is the sound of television in Spanish. Children in Argentina enjoy watching

A young girl in Patagonia feeds an armadillo that stops by her door at dinnertime.

television, and adults often watch *novelas*, ongoing soap operas, which are broadcast from morning to evening. The most popular program on Argentine television, without a doubt, is soccer.

The Tradition of Mate

Argentines like to invite friends and neighbors to their homes for small parties or just to spend the evening with the family. They enjoy their tradition of *hospitalidad*, or hospitality, and one way they show friendship is to offer guests mate, a slightly bitter herb tea. Mate must be served in a certain way. A few pinches of the crumpled green-gray leaves—which have been handpicked and dried for up to ten years—are put into a dried gourd (also called a mate). This gourd is then filled with boiling water, allowed to sit a moment, and passed around from person to person. The tea is sipped through bombillas, or metal straws. Argentines are very proud of their mate gourds, which are decorated with etchings or silverwork. Shops have dozens of different kinds for sale.

Argentine families often gather in the kitchen, where a television program might be playing while several conversations take place. Although this sounds confusing, Argentines often protest, in fun, that two ears can be trained to do the work of four! They are likely to discuss

Argentines enjoying a Saturday morning breakfast of rolls and mate–their country's traditional beverage

important issues—where jobs are scarce, for example, young adults might talk about moving to mineral-rich Patagonia to find work. Almost everyone will want to give an opinion. Argentines value the ability to express themselves; during these discussions, children learn to say what they think.

Changing Roles for Women

Fathers in Argentina have traditionally been considered the head of the family, or *hombre de familia*.

The traditional mother was in charge of the household, *mujer de su casa*. Argentine mothers and grandmothers have always been given an affectionate respect. At family gatherings, there is a lot of teasing that, *Es la mujer la jefa* ("The woman is the boss"). In the past, women were expected to be gentle and modest, listen to their husband's opinions, raise a large family, cook meals, and represent the family at church.

Today more than half the women in urban areas work, earning money of their own, and they consider those ideas old-fashioned. Argentine women are now a strong force in the workplace. Yet women often consider their husbands the final authority in family matters even today.

At one time, married children lived with their parents in a new section that was built onto the house. Today young married couples usually find their own apartments, but they still keep in close contact with their families. Weddings, baptisms, parties, and holidays are times when the whole family gets together. Relatives help each other by lending money or tools, by babysitting, or by helping during an illness.

Argentine Meals

In Argentine families, everyone is likely to be on a different schedule. If the mother does not work outside the home, she sometimes cooks separate meals for each person. Most Argentines rise early and work late, with a few hours off in the afternoon to nap. *Desayuno*, or breakfast, is a light meal of rolls, or jam and bread, with coffee and sometimes fruit. Workers in the country usually eat a larger breakfast, sometimes including meat. At midmorning, mate is served with a snack such as a meat-stuffed pastry.

Lunch, or *almuerzo*, is usually eaten at noon or 1:00 P.M. Working people in the cities and most rural people have small lunches. Lunch for an Argentine office worker might be a slice of pizza at a cafeteria; a farmworker's midday meal, carried hot to the field in a terra-cotta dish, could be a stew of minced beef, potatoes, and corncob chunks. Upper-class city families often follow past traditions more closely, and they might eat a hearty midday meal with meat, potatoes, and green vegetables.

Most shops close from 12:30 P.M. until 4:00 P.M. Some people use this time to take a *siesta*, or nap, because they woke up early and will stay up late. About 5:00 P.M, *confiterías*, or tearooms—a tradition introduced by the British—fill up with people having a snack of tea, sandwiches, and cake to tide them over until a late dinner, or *cena*. Dinner is a substantial meal of several courses, usually with a meat dish. It may not be served until 9:00 P.M or later.

Huge cuts of beef roast over an open fire in an Argentine barbecue.

Beef on Horseback

Argentina's national dish is *bife*, or beef. Argentines enjoy eating it rare or—as they say—*pero no blu*, which is similar to the expression "rare but not mooing"! Many Argentines try to eat beef at every meal, and they have many different ways to prepare it. *Asado* is a beef roast cooked over an open fire. Steak topped with an egg is called *bife a caballo* (beef on horseback). *Parrillada* is blood sausages, ribs, and other cuts of meat grilled together, and *churrasco* is grilled steak. *Milanesa* is beef dipped in egg and crumbs, and then fried. Many restaurants also offer *asado con cuero*, a whole steer roasted in its natural state, complete with hide and hair.

Because many Argentines are descended from Italian immigrants, Italian food is also popular. Pizza is sold throughout the country, along with pastas of all sorts: tortelli, tortellini, spaghetti, capeletti, lasagna, and canelloni. Children enjoy Italian favorites such as *ñoquis,* potato dumplings with tomato sauce and meat, and Italian- style ice cream cones served in two flavors.

Argentines eat more fruit than people in any other country—233 pounds (106 kilograms) per person in an average year. Peaches, apricots, plums, quinces, pears, cherries, and grapes are favorites, along with apples from the Río Negro area and oranges, grapefruit, lemons, and tangerines from Mesopotamia. *Tuna,* the fruit of the prickly pear cactus, is also popular.

Locro is a stew made with corn, beans, boiled meat, and pumpkins. Another stew is *carbonada,* which is cooked in a clay pan over a slow fire. It has meat, pumkins, potatoes, sweet potatoes, and chunks of corn on the cob. *Puchero de gallina* is a stew made from chicken pieces, sausage, corn, and squash.

The little pies called empanadas are usually stuffed with beef, but they can be made with chicken, seafood, vegetables, or even pumpkin. Empanadas are held in the hand while being eaten. To make this favorite Argentine snack, remember to mix the dough with your hands. Stirring with spoons is not allowed!

Empanadas

Filling
1 pound hamburger meat
1/2 cup chopped onions
8 chopped green olives
1 teaspoon salt
1/4 teaspoon oregano

Cook the hamburger and onions in a frying pan. Stir in the other ingredients. Drain the meat mixture on a paper towel. Set it aside to cool.

Pastry
2 1/2 cups flour
1 egg yolk
1/2 cup water (approximately)
1/4 cup butter
1 teaspoon vinegar
1/2 teaspoon salt

In a bowl, mix together the flour, butter, egg yolk, and vinegar, using your hands. Stir the salt into the water and sprinkle it, a little at a time, over the flour mixture. Knead the dough until it is smooth and stiff.

For each empanada, roll 1/4 cup of dough into a 9-inch circle, put 1/2 cup of filling on the circle, and fold it in half. Press the edges of the dough together with your fingers. Poke with a toothpick. Bake on a cookie sheet in a 400-degree oven for 10 to 15 minutes. Serve hot.

For dessert, Argentine children often ask their mothers to make *dulce de leche* which looks like butterscotch pudding. It's easy to make, and just right to satisfy a sweet tooth.

Dulce de Leche

1 can sweetened condensed milk

Pour the can of sweetened condensed milk into an 8-inch glass pie pan, and cover it with foil. Place the pie pan in a shallow pan filled with one inch of water. Bake for one hour in a 425-degree oven.

Dulce de leche is often eaten spread over buttered toast. It can also be made into sandwiches, spread like frosting on cakes, or eaten with bananas. *Buen Apetito!*

RESPECT FOR LEARNING

There is one block in Buenos Aires that is called *la manzana de las luces*, or the "city block of learning." In the many buildings on this block are thousands and thousands of books. Here are the city's oldest bookstores, the department where books and educational materials are chosen for use in the country's public schools, the original city library, a small Jesuit college, and the Natural History Museum of Argentina. Many of these buildings are as old as the city itself—Argentines have had the desire to be educated since the country began.

Most Argentines try to make learning part of their daily lives. They value education and enjoy reading. In fact, about 94 percent of all Argentines can read and write. Many Argentine universities are more than three hundred years old—the oldest, in Córdoba, was built in 1613. The people are proud of the five Nobel prizes awarded to Argentine scientists, diplomats, and human rights activists in the twentieth century. The Argentines who cannot read and write live mainly in isolated rural areas, especially in the northern provinces, where getting to school can be a problem.

Most Argentine young people, though, live in cities or towns near schools, and most Argentine families earn

Education can begin early in Argentina. These young children play at a kindergarten.

enough money to provide the uniforms, books, and transportation their children need to attend school. Adequate incomes mean that fewer children must be kept out of school to work and help support the family. Because a high percentage of Argentine adults are educated, they want their children to go to school as well.

Public and Private Schools

Argentine parents face many choices throughout their children's education. Children aged four and five may attend kindergarten in either public or private schools, but parents do not have to send their children to school at this age. Kindergarten children follow the Argentine tradition of wearing school uniforms—instead of the white uniforms older students wear, kindergartners dress in pink or pastel colors.

Beginning when they are six years old, Argentine children must attend seven years of primary school. All public primary schools are free, although parents may choose to send their children to private schools, which may be sponsored by churches or organizations. Private schools can be very expensive. Not all families can afford them, but some people believe their children will get a better education in private school.

Argentine primary school is divided into first grade, second grade, and so on, similar to schools in the United States. What the students learn is decided by the Argentine National Council of Education, and both private and public schools must follow its plan. All classes are taught in Spanish, except in private schools, where the children of foreign workers or students need to have only half the day's instruction in Spanish. Public primary schools also teach a foreign language, usually English, at a very simple level. In private schools, a foreign language—often English or French—is also taught.

Students in primary school study reading, mathematics, science, history, and art. In the past, students learned by memorizing facts, but that has changed, and today students learn by watching demonstrations and practicing skills, as well as memorizing.

The school year opens in March and ends in December. All students start and finish classes in those months, except for university students and some students in remote areas. The Argentine government has a separate program for educating mentally or physically disabled children at primary and upper levels.

The School Day

There are no public school buses in Argentina, so boys and girls in primary school may begin the day by walking to school if they live near enough. If they don't, their father or mother might drive them, or they might ride the subway or take a city bus. Students arrive on the school grounds dressed in their uniforms—white button-in-the-back dresses and knee-high socks for girls, and white jackets and dark pants, often jeans, for boys. Uniforms are worn so that children from poorer families will not dress differently from those whose families are wealthy.

Students carry their books and supplies in backpacks, and the pockets of their uniforms are often bulging with snacks and other necessities. Unlike schools in North America, in Argentina the family must pay for the

Students at public high schools are required to wear white uniforms.

student's textbooks—the school does not furnish them. As a result, even young children learn that they must not lose their books. Textbooks and uniforms can be expensive for poorer families, especially if they have several children of school age.

Primary students in Argentina go to school for fewer hours than North American students do. The school day is run in two split shifts, with four hours in each shift. Students attend classes either from 8:00 A.M. until noon or from 1:00 P.M. until 5:00 P.M. All of a student's classes are held in the same room, even in high school. When the bell rings, the teachers move from room to room, not the students.

During the split shifts there are usually three ten-minute recesses from class. For kindergartners and some primary students, this means *merienda*—a snack, usually milk and a small roll similar to a donut hole. Physical education is taught twice a week and provides another chance to work off excess energy. Students look forward to the occasional field trip to a museum, puppet play, or concert.

Making Choices

Argentine public high schools are free, but almost half of the country's high schools are private institutions that charge tuition. Students enter high school when they finish primary school, usually at fourteen or fifteen years of age, but a few are as young as eleven or twelve. One out of every five students is between eighteen and twenty-four years old—older than most North American high school students. Most of these students left high school when they were younger for financial reasons, and they have now returned to finish their studies. The government has urged older students to go back to school, and the plan has worked fairly well.

High school students have a longer school day of six or seven hours. In high school, young Argentines take more classes than North American students—sometimes as many as ten different classes.

Argentine high schools give students many choices in their education. In the United States, students usually take four years to finish high school, but Argentine students can take between five and seven years to complete a program that varies depending on the courses the student has chosen. All high school students must complete certain basic courses, and then they may find themselves making some difficult decisions.

Students who want to attend a university after high school take classes to earn a *bachillerato* certificate, a five-year program. Students who do not want university training can choose career training in a trade such as agriculture, art, weaving, dressmaking, cooking, and other skills. Young people might also choose to earn a *técnico*, or technical degree. They study automotive mechanics, electronics, or other technical skills that will help them earn a living. High school students have yet another option—those who wish to may study both a university and a technical course.

Some high school students, especially older ones with families of their own, may drop out of school because they need to work to earn money. The government provides night classes for these students. This is the long way to finish high school, though—a student in night classes may take up to eight years to finish technical training.

High school girls learn to sew as part of a technical program.

Higher Education

The best Argentine students can choose to attend an institution of higher education after finishing high school. There are forty-eight universities in Argentina. More than half of them are public schools, supported by the government, where students attend free of charge. With an enrollment of more than 140,000 students, the University of Buenos Aires is the largest university on the South American continent. Students come from other Latin American countries to study there and in Argentina's many other universities. The nation also has many fine institutions of higher education for training teachers, sports instructors, and artists.

The number of Argentine students attending universities is growing rapidly and is expected to keep rising. During the 1970s the military government had limited the number of students who could enter universities, cut back on spending for education, censored books, and persecuted professors for their ideas. Today half a million Argentine students attend universities and special schools of higher education every year.

Unusual Schools

Some Argentine schools are very unusual because of where they are or what they look like. Extremely large ranches may have their own one-room schools with a single teacher in charge. Such rural schools can suffer from a lack of funds when the wealthy landowners in the area live far away from their land and do not feel a need to support the school. Low prices for a region's main product, such as beef or sugar, mean less money for country schools, too. Rural students also occasionally get to school in an unusual way—riding horseback.

Most city schools in Argentina look alike with rows of desks and blackboards, but primary students in La Boca, an older section of Buenos Aires, can attend classes in a most unusual school. In this out-of-the-ordinary school, blackboards are not black, but green,

Young children play on playground equipment in colorful La Boca.

pink, and yellow, and walls are decorated in bright patterns and artistic displays.

Even though these children learn in unusual surroundings, they are very much like all students in Argentina. And with their parents' help they will have to make many educational choices during their school years.

A LOVE OF SPORTS

Argentines often spend their free time in one of two ways—either watching or playing sports. The capital city, it is said, has more sports fields than any other city in the world. Porteños enjoy spending their time at the city's many arenas, where spectator sports draw huge crowds of loyal fans. Buenos Aires has an *hipódromo* for horseracing and an *autódromo* for auto racing. For soccer—the number-one team sport in the country—there is no single arena but about twenty stadiums.

Fútbol Fever

Argentines love *fútbol*, as soccer is called. British sailors brought the sport to Argentina in the late nineteenth century, and it quickly became popular. When the Argentine national team won their second World Cup championship on June 29, 1986, in Mexico City with a 3–2 victory over West Germany, fans in the stadium went wild with excitement, stamping their feet and yelling. Some even painted their faces blue and white, the Argentine national colors. At home, millions of people watched the match on television, and for that moment the nation was united in pride. All the members of the team

Professional soccer games, such as this one in Buenos Aires, draw thousands of enthusiastic Argentine fans.

became instant heroes and were honored with a parade when they returned to Buenos Aires. One restaurant there even named a sandwich after each team member.

Argentine soccer fans can be very emotional about their teams. They chant, shout, and whistle throughout the matches, sometimes insulting the fans cheering for the other side. Typically, only men and boys attend soccer matches; the game is not popular with women and girls, and there are no organized teams for women or girls in the country.

On Saturday afternoons and whenever they have free time, boys gather to play fútbol in parks, on soccer fields, or on city streets. They may play in organized leagues or informally with friends. A boy's soccer ball is often his favorite possession, and even very young boys practice moving and passing the ball with their feet. Boys often dream of playing for the "first division," or major league, teams when they are old enough.

Soccer is played year-round throughout the country. First-division games are usually held on Sunday afternoons and may be attended by as many as 120,000 fans at Río Plate Stadium in Buenos Aires. In Argentina, first-division teams are each owned by a different social-athletic club, and each club maintains its own stadium. Argentines must pay dues to belong to these clubs, but they take pride in supporting a winning team. Clubs also support many other sports in Argentina.

People in La Boca can be especially enthusiastic fans of their team, the Boca Juniors, particularly when the match is with their biggest rivals, the Río Plate team. The Boca Juniors play in a stadium called *La Bombónera*, which means "the candy box." Soccer is such a common topic of conversation that on the day of a match, porteños may even ask strangers, "Boca or Plate?" to satisfy their curiosity about what team that person supports. They assume that most people are interested in fútbol, and most Argentines are!

Sports on Horseback

Second only to soccer in popularity are sports that feature horseback riding. Many Argentines are fine riders, a tradition that stems from the country's wild west heritage. Riding skills were important to the gauchos and Indians who tamed the wild horses of the pampas. Today Argentine horses are among the best in the world, with bloodlines from the finest stock. At one time wealthy Argentines traveled the world to find magnificent horses for their stables. Argentina's limestone rich soil builds strong bones in thoroughbreds, and the country has vast pastures for horses to run in. Some U.S. Triple Crown horse racing champions were the descendants of Argentine horses.

On weekends and holidays, porteños flock to the dirt racetrack at the government-owned Hipódromo in Palermo Park for horse racing. Argentines like to wager, and they buy tickets in packets of ten to place bets on their favorite horses. At the sidelines, bettors can even buy lists of "guaranteed" winners! Money that the government earns from betting goes to charity.

Another popular horseback sport is *pato*, which is like a mixture of basketball and polo. This sport was invented in Argentina and is not played anywhere else in the world. In Spanish, *pato* means "duck." Gauchos used to stuff a live duck into a bag, with its head poking out. Two teams on horseback struggled over the bag, trying to score by tossing it through a big basket. The game was forbidden in the early nineteenth century because it often became violent, but President Juan Manuel de Rosas was enthusiastic about gaucho games and brought it back. Today a big, six-handled ball has replaced the unfortunate duck, and the Argentine Pato Federation organizes clubs to play the game.

Polo, played mostly by the wealthy, is a popular spectator sport. Argentine polo teams have won a number of Olympic gold medals, and they are highly respected on the international circuit. The Argentine Open Championship and the Americas Cup are important polo events held in Buenos Aires. Ranked the best player in the world, Gonzolo Pieres is a national hero. Most of Argentina's 6,000 registered players are men, but women and youngsters also compete in their own tournaments.

Mountaineering

In Argentina, mountaineering is called *alpinismo*,

An exciting polo match in Buenos Aires

which includes skiing and hiking as well as mountain climbing. These sports are very popular with young people and university students. During the early twentieth century, Argentine students in Europe first tried winter sports in the Alps; when they returned home to Argentina, they began practicing these activities in the Andes. A group of these students later started Club Andinos. Today this organization is made up of thousands of volunteers who give their time to build shelters on snowy trails for skiers and climbers, and arrange skiing competitions. Their shelters have saved many lives.

Aconcagua, the tallest mountain outside Asia, has become a special target for mountain climbers from all over the world. Early climbers were forced to turn back because of harsh cold, falling rocks, fast-breaking storms, and nausea from altitude sickness, but today's climbers use lightweight clothing, weather information, and special equipment to make the climb safer and easier. Club Andinos has built shelters every 1,000 feet (305 meters) as well. The summer month of January is popular with groups that plan to climb South America's highest mountain.

Many Argentine families take winter skiing vacations, and most ski areas have "family" apartments to rent. Skiing became very popular after the World Cup downhill events were staged in the mid-1980s at Las Lenas, an Andean mountain resort south of Mendoza. During ski lessons, lines of children follow instructors down small hills. Very young children, grandparents, and other family members who don't ski often come along on ski vacations, too. They may ride the ski lift to the mountaintop and relax inside the lodge near a fireplace, sipping hot chocolate and eating cigar-sized *churros* (fried pastry) as they watch skiers navigate the ridges of snow.

Skiing of another kind is popular on Tierra del Fuego—cross-country skiing. At Ushuaia, Club Andinos members can go cross-country skiing on a trail that passes by beaver lodges and fox tracks.

Argentines enjoy the beautiful sandy beaches at Mar del Plata.

Families on Vacation

Argentines often say that there are no worries in Argentina in January because everybody is at the beach! Although Buenos Aires is located on the shores of the Atlantic Ocean, it isn't a beach town. When porteños and other Argentines want sandy beaches, they travel to Mar del Plata to swim and sunbathe. Vacationers stay in waterside hotels or campgrounds, and change into their swimsuits at the beach inside a *carpa*, a seaside tent.

Families usually vacation during the summer months of January and February, or during the three-week school holiday in July. Some may go to hotels or camps that are owned and operated by labor unions for the use of their members. Here, fees for weeklong stays are very low, costing little more than staying at home. Other campgrounds are open to the public. The lakes in the southern Andes and the hills near Córdoba attract campers, who set up tents and barbecue meat on grills.

Water sports such as boating and fishing are popular with Argentines who live near lakes or rivers. At Chascomús, a lake 80 miles (129 kilometers) from the capital, whole families fish in the musty-smelling waters for *pejerrey*, a kind of catfish. On Tierra del Fuego and along the coast of Patagonia, boys and girls hunt the windswept, rocky beaches to find the *delfíns* (dolphins) and whales that sometimes wash ashore. Community groups help these beached sea animals, if they can. Tierra del Fuego is also known for its giant brown trout, which migrate up the Río Grande from the Atlantic Ocean to spawn.

Sports Heroes

Argentina has produced many world champions in tennis, boxing, gymnastics, swimming, and other non-team sports. Because many of these champions have become national heroes and role models, these sports have also become popular with Argentine children and young adults. Many girls in Argentina practice gymnastics, and both boys and girls learn to play tennis. Even as children, many energetic young Argentines are sports-minded. They enjoy playing sports and show a desire to win.

Gabriela Sabatini is an Argentine tennis star who ranks among the top female tennis players in the world. Sabatini began playing in international tennis competitions at age fifteen and has played at Wimbledon and in the French Open Tournament. She won a silver medal at the 1988 Summer Olympics. Although young fans admire and try to copy her, her own hero is her countryman Guillermo Vilas, a tennis superstar of the 1970s.

In 1994, Juan Coggi won the World Boxing Association championship in the junior welterweight division. He is one of a long line of Argentine boxers to hold world titles. Argentines first became interested in boxing in the 1920s with the "Wild Bull of the Pampas," as boxer Luis Angel Firpo was called. In 1923, Firpo knocked world heavyweight champion Jack Dempsey over the ropes and out of the ring. Although Firpo later lost the match to Dempsey, he represents the "fight to win" spirit of many Argentine sports heroes.

Just for Fun

How young people have fun in Argentina may depend on where they live and what they can afford to spend. In the cities, many kinds of recreation are available; in rural areas there are fewer organized activities. Young Argentines enjoy seeing the latest movies, visiting friends, watching soccer on television, renting movie videos, or just walking with friends, talking and window-shopping. They might also pay a visit to a miniature store called a *kiosco* for soft drinks or cider. Parks are popular with young people because they often have swimming pools and areas for picnicking. Children may play *escondida*, or hide-and-seek, among the trees and shrubs, ride handcranked carousels, or visit a zoo within a park. Like other Argentines, they try not to miss a chance to have fun, whether it's watching or playing sports, or going on vacations.

Argentine tennis star Gabriela Sabatini

ARGENTINES ABROAD

In general, Argentina is a country that people move to rather than leave. Over the past century, six million people have immigrated to Argentina, nearly all from Europe. Immigrants from neighboring South American countries have also found new homes in this large nation. With its untapped natural resources and unpopulated open spaces, Argentina is viewed as a "land of opportunity" much the same as the United States.

Yet some people do leave Argentina in search of new and better lives. During the years before World War II, thousands of Argentines gave up their citizenship and left the country. Most were not native-born Argentines, but had come to the country full of hope for a better life. They moved on again, without having found a comfortable place in Argentine society.

The Brain Drain

Another group of Argentines moved to the United States during the 1950s, 1960s, and 1970s. Unlike people who had left Argentina before World War II, these were native-born Argentines. The number leaving was not large, but many of the emigrants were professional people such as doctors, engineers, chemists, accountants, dentists, and technicians. Because people in these professions often make research discoveries or help care for the health of a country's citizens, Argentine officials became concerned. This emigration came to be called the Brain Drain.

Many of the doctors and other professionals who left the country during this time did so because there were not enough jobs for them. Professors from Argentine universities sometimes left too but for another reason—to escape the military government then in power that jailed or killed some educators. The United States was the destination most often chosen by these skilled workers leaving their country.

Those who stayed in Argentina found that their lives improved when the country returned to a democratic government in 1983. In the 1980s fewer Argentines from all walks of life, including skilled people, emigrated to the United States, and the Brain Drain was declared over. All together, about 80,000 Argentines—both skilled and unskilled—left their homeland to come to the United States between 1961 and the late 1980s. The number may not be large compared to the number of people who came to the United States from several other Latin American countries during this same time, but it includes many talented people.

Swallows

Argentine Americans love their homeland and may think of returning there with their families to live. Shortly after the Brain Drain, the Gillette Foundation, a private research group, asked 4,000 Argentine Americans in the United States, "Would you go back to Argentina if you had a job there?" The majority answered yes. Jobs in Argentina were arranged for those who wanted to return, and hundreds of educated Argentine Americans took advantage of the opportunity to return to their homeland.

Because they considered both the United States and Argentina their homes, the people who returned called themselves "swallows," after the famous birds that Argentina and the United States share, the swallows of San Juan Capistrano. These birds migrate with the seasons. They spend the summer (which is winter in North America) in Argentina, and then fly north to the United States for the summer months there. The swallows nearly always arrive in California on the same day, March 19, at an old Spanish mission called San Juan Capistrano. Crowds of people wait to see the first swallows arrive from their long journey.

For years, Argentina has graciously shared the talents of one special man with the United States and the world. Like the swallows, Dante Caputo has divided his time between Argentina and the United States.

Dante Caputo

He studied at the University of Buenos Aires in Argentina, as well as at Harvard and Tufts universities in the United States. Later he was president of the forty-third session of the General Assembly of the United Nations, in New York City, and also Minister of Foreign Relations and Worship for the government of Argentina. Today he lives in Buenos Aires, traveling abroad as an unofficial spokesman for his homeland.

Movie Stars and Musical Rhythms

Members of the Lamas family are Argentine Americans who are well known in the Hollywood entertainment industry. Two generations of this talented family have worked in movies and television as actors and directors. The father, Fernando Lamas, was born in Buenos Aires in 1915 and emigrated to the United States as a young man. He first acted in Spanish language films in the 1940s, but his talent for playing handsome leading men was quickly discovered, and he became known as the silvery Argentine. Fernando's movies had exciting titles such as *Kill a Dragon, Valley of Mysteries*, and *The Revenge of the Musketeers*. Later Fernando Lamas progressed from being a movie actor to being a movie director.

Today, Lamas's son, Lorenzo, is a second-generation Argentine American who works in the world of television and action-adventure movies. Lorenzo stars in the popular television series, *Renegade*, and like his father, he plays a leading man. Lorenzo is also a race car driver and participates in the martial arts.

In the 1930s many Hollywood movies vibrated with the rhythmic sound of the tango. Today some movie scores still feature the color and flair of Argentina's most famous musical export. Most Americans may think of the tango first when they think of Argentine music. Someone who dances the tango or listens to tango music is taking part in

Popular Argentine American television star Lorenzo Lamas

an Argentine contribution to the world.

People of Argentine heritage have also brought their own style of classical music to the United States. The world-famous conductor and pianist Daniel Barenboim was born in Buenos Aires in 1942. A child star, he was just seven years old when he made his debut playing the piano in Argentina. Barenboim now lives in the United States, where he brings an Argentine flavor to his important work—conducting the Chicago Symphony Orchestra.

Argentine-born Julio Bocca is an energetic young ballet dancer and an international star. His grace and skill won him the prized Medal of Moscow award. Bocca has lived in New York City and danced with the American Ballet Theater there. Though he travels the world to perform on grand stages, Bocca learned to dance, as a young boy, at the Colon Theater of Buenos Aires, and today he appears there as often as he can.

Medical Research

The physicians, chemists, engineers, and other trained professionals who left Argentina during the Brain Drain have given the United States some wide-ranging advances in research, especially in the field of medicine. Many people around the world have benefited from the life-saving research conducted by these emigrants. Argentine

Americans are known for their research in infertility, heart disease, cancer, and many other medical areas.

One Argentine-American researcher is Dr. Rene Geronimo Favaloro, who is famous for his work on heart bypass surgery. He was the first surgeon to replace a patient's diseased heart arteries with a leg vein that could carry blood around the blocked areas to the heart. Favaloro was born in the city of La Plata, south of Buenos Aires. As a young doctor, he conducted medical research in the United States. Today he spends time in the United States, where he is a medical consultant, and in Argentina, where he is director of the Institute of Cardiology in Buenos Aires.

Maintaining Ties

In some ways, many Argentine immigrants have had an advantage in adjusting to life in the United States. Because English is a common second language in Argentina, especially in urban areas, Argentine Americans may face less of a language barrier than other immigrants. Many are also professional people who may have found it easier to obtain a job. Finally, because Argentina and the United States were both settled mainly by Europeans, the two countries have many similarities in outlook, such as admiration for the contribution of the individual.

Argentine Americans tend to maintain contact with each other to share news of their homeland. Several U.S. cities have large Argentine communities. New York City alone has about 40,000 Argentine Americans. Many of them live in the Jackson Heights area, where there are Argentine-style bakeries, restaurants, newsstands, butcher shops, as well as stores that sell Argentine-made items.

Many Argentine Americans are proud of their homeland, and they try to keep their heritage alive through organizations. In Washington, D.C., the sizable community of Argentine Americans supports an organization named the San Martín Society. Members of this organization gather to remember the contributions of General José de San Martín to the liberation of Argentina from Spanish rule. Other organizations, such as the Argentine-North American Association for the Advancement of Science, Technology, and Culture, located in New York City, help Argentine Americans in their careers.

The contributions of Argentine Americans are woven into the fabric of American life in the same way that wool yarn is woven into an Argentine poncho. Some contributions are gifts that respond to human

A meeting of the San Martín Society in Washington, D.C.

needs such as saving or prolonging lives through medical research. Others are gifts that bring joy and pleasure—the dramatic movements of the tango or an original interpretation of classical music. The Argentines in the United States are not a large group, but their talents, along with those of other groups of American immigrants, have enriched the culture of their adopted home.

Appendix

Argentine Embassies and Consulates in the United States and Canada

Argentine embassies and consulates offer information and assistance to Americans and Canadians who want to learn about Argentina or visit there. Contact the embassy or consulate nearest you for more information.

U.S. Embassy and Consulate

New York, New York
Argentine Consulate General
12 W. 56th St.
New York, NY 10019
Phone (212) 603-0400

Washington, D.C.
Argentine Embassy
1600 New Hampshire Ave., N.W.
Washington, D.C. 20009
Phone (202) 939-6400

Canadian Embassy and Consulate

Montreal, Quebec
Argentine Consulate
2000 Beel St., Rm. 710
Montreal, Quebec H3A 2W5
Phone (514) 842-3369

Ottawa, Ontario
Argentine Embassy
910-90 Sparks St.
Ottawa, Ontario K1P 5B4
Phone (613) 236-2351

GLOSSARY

almuerzo (ahl MWAIR soh)—lunch

alpinismo (ahl pee NEES moh)—the sports of skiing, hiking, and mountain climbing

asado (ah SAH doh)—a beef roast cooked over an open fire

asado con cuero (ah SAH doh kohn koo EH roh)—a whole steer roasted in its hide

autódromo (ow TOH droh moh)—a track for auto racing

bachillerato (bah chee sheh RAH toh)—a high school degree given to students who intend to attend a university

bandoneón (bahn doh nee OHN)—an accordion-like instrument used to play tango music

bife (BEE feh)—beef

bife a caballo (BEE fay ah kah BAH shoh)—steak topped with an egg

boleadoras (boh lee ah DOH rahs)—a weapon made of several stones joined together by leather strips

bombachas (bohm BAH chahs)—baggy pants worn by gauchos

bombilla (bohm BEE shah)—a silver straw used to drink an herb tea called *mate*

buen apetito (bwehn ah puh TEE toh)—good appetite; a phrase used at the beginning of a meal

carnavalito (kahr nah vah LEE toh)—a centuries-old Indian dance

carpa (KAHR pah)—a seaside tent

caudillo   (kow DEE shoh)—a rich landowner from
the provinces

cena (SEH nah)—dinner or supper

churrasco (choo RAHS koh)—grilled beefsteak

churro (CHOO roh)—fried pastry

colectivo (koh lek TEE voh)—a Buenos Aires bus

confiterías (kohn fee teh REE ahs)—tearooms

delfín (dehl FEEN)—dolphin

desayuno (deh sah ZHOO noh)—breakfast

los desaparecidos (lohs dehs ah pahr eh SEE dohs)—the
missing; people who disappeared during the military
leadership of the 1970s and early 1980s

dulce de leche (DUL seh deh LEH cheh)—a dessert
made from milk and sugar

empanada (ehm pah NAH dah)—a little pastry stufffed
with meat, seafood, vegetables, or fruit

en casa (ehn KAH sah)—at home

escondida (ehs kohn DEE dah)—the children's game of
hide-and-seek

escondido (ehs kohn DEE doh)—a gaucho folk dance

estancia (ehs TAHN see ah)—a ranch

familia (fa MEE lee yah)—family

fiesta (fee EHS tah)—a celebration

fuegos artificiales   (foo EH gohs   ahr tee fee SEE-
ahl ehs)—fireworks

fútbol (FUT bohl)—soccer

gaucho (GOW choh)—an Argentine cowboy

los gringos locos (lohs GREEN gohs loh kohs)—the crazy foreigners

guanaco (wah NAH koh)—a llama-like animal related to the camel

hipódromo (ee POH droh moh)—a horseracing track

hombre de familia (OHM breh deh fam MEE lee yah)—the man who heads the family

hospitalidad (ohs pee tah lee DAHD)—hospitality

kiosco (KYAHS koh)—a miniature store

mara (MAH ra)—a short-eared rabbit

mate (MAH teh)—an herb tea drunk from a gourd with a metal straw; also the name of the gourd

merienda (meh ree EHN dah)—a snack eaten during a break in the school day

mestizo (mehs TEE soh)—a person of mixed European and Indian background

milanesa (mee lah NEH sah)—thin slices of beef, coated in crumbs and fried

mujer de su casa (moo HEHR deh soo KAH sah)—mother of the house, or housewife

ñoquis (NYOH kees)—potato dumplings with tomato sauce and meat

novela (noh VAY lah)—a televised soap opera

pampas (PAHM pahs)—the grassy plains of the Pampa

pampero (pahm PEH roh)—a windstorm that moves across the Pampa

pan dulce (pahn DUL seh)—a sweet bread with dried fruits and nuts, eaten at Christmas

parrillada (pah ree SHAH dah)— sausages, ribs, and other cuts of meat grilled together

pato (PAH toh)—a game played on horseback using a six-handled ball; also means "duck"

patrón (pah TROHN)—a wealthy landowner who commanded the loyalty of gauchos

pejerrey (peh HEH ray)—a kind of catfish

pero no blu (PEH roh noh bloo)—similar to the expression "rare but not mooing"; it describes how Argentines like to eat beef

porteños (pohr tehn yohs)—people from the port, the name used for the residents of Buenos Aires

pulperías (pool peh REE ahs)—gaucho saloons where the tango was born

quebracho (keh BRAH choh)—a hardwood tree, nicknamed the ax breaker

rancho (RAHN choh)—a rural worker's modest home

siesta (see EHS tah)—a nap during a break from work

técnico (TEHK nee koh)—a technical degree earned in high school

tuna (TOO nah)—the fruit from a cactus

vicuña (vee KOO nyah)—a llama-like animal

villas miserias (VEE shus mee SEH ree ahs)—slums

yerba mate (ZHER bah MAH teh)—a holly shrub

zamba (SAHM bah)—a handkerchief dance

SELECTED BIBLIOGRAPHY

Ball, Deirdre, ed. *Argentina*. Singapore: Höfer Communications Ltd., 1994.

Cameron, Ian. *Magellan*. New York: Saturday Review Press, 1973.

Chatwin, Bruce. *In Patagonia*. New York: Summit Books, 1977.

Freedman, Lawrence. "The War of the Falklands Islands." *Foreign Affairs* (Fall, 1982): 204–209.

Harris, Graham. "A Patagonian Family Album." *Animal Kingdom* (January/February, 1989): 12–17.

Hintz, Martin. *Argentina*. Chicago: Childrens Press, 1985.

Pimlott, John. *South and Central America*. New York: Aladdin Books Ltd., 1987.

Raymont, Henry, ed. *The Liberator: General San Martín*. Washington, DC: Organization of the American States Printing Office, 1978.

Rodgers, Mary M., ed. *Argentina in Pictures*. Minneapolis, MN: Lerner Publications, 1988.

Rudolph, James. *Argentina: A Country Study*. Washington, DC: U.S. Government Printing Office, 1986.

Wheaten, Kathleen, ed. *Buenos Aires*. Boston: Houghton Mifflin, 1994.

INDEX

ABOUT THE AUTHORS

The daughter of an Argentine American, Marge Peterson and her husband, Rob, have traveled in Argentina and other South American countries. Marge is a free-lance writer and former fourth- and fifth-grade teacher with a Master's degree in education. Rob is a Fulbright Scholar with a Ph.D. in international business who currently teaches at New Mexico State University. The Petersons have published more than one hundred magazine articles, and Rob is the author of seven nonfiction books.

    The Petersons have two children and live in Las Cruces, New Mexico.